Lightning at Dinner

:::

Other Books by Jim Moore

The New Body

What the Bird Sees

How We Missed Belgium
(with Deborah Keenan)

The Freedom of History

The Long Experience of Love

Writing with Tagore

Minnesota Writes Anthology (co-editor)

LIGHTNING AT DINNER

poems by

Jim Moore

Graywolf Press
Saint Paul, Minnesota

Publication of this volume is made possible in part by a grant provided by the Minnesota State Arts Board, through an appropriation by the Minnesota State Legislature; a grant from the Wells Fargo Foundation Minnesota; and a grant from the National Endowment for the Arts, which believes that a great nation deserves great art. Significant support has also been provided by the Bush Foundation; Target and Mervyn's with support from the Target Foundation; the McKnight Foundation; and other generous contributions from foundations, corporations, and individuals. To these organizations and individuals we offer our heartfelt thanks.

Published by Graywolf Press
2402 University Avenue, Suite 203
Saint Paul, Minnesota 55114
All rights reserved.

www.graywolfpress.org

Published in the United States of America

ISBN 1-55597-425-2

2   4   6   8   9   7   5   3

Library of Congress Control Number: 2004116117

Cover design: Craig Davidson
Cover photograph: *Pitcher,* JoAnn Verburg © 1997

Acknowledgments

Grateful acknowledgement is made to the following magazines where a number of these poems first appeared, and especially to *Water~Stone* for its continuing faith in my work:

The Bloomsbury Review
Luna
The New Yorker
North Stone Review
Speakeasy
ThreeCandles.com
The Threepenny Review
Water~Stone

"It Is Hard Not to Love the World" was reprinted from *Water~Stone* in Volume XXVI of *The Pushcart Prize Anthology*.

I also acknowledge with much gratitude a Loft McKnight grant in poetry that helped in the completion of these poems.

Thanks to all my steadfast friends in poetry who have read this book at crucial times, and especially to Michael Dennis Browne, Carol Conroy, Jane Hilberry, Lewis Hyde, Deborah Keenan, Patricia Kirkpatrick, David Mason, Bart Schneider, and JoAnn Verburg.

I also want to particularly thank Fiona McCrae at Graywolf for her warm welcome to the book and initial insightful editing.

William Maxwell writes that "editors work close to the page, obsessed with whether or not the writer has said what he meant to say." This is exactly what Jeff Shotts did when he stepped in as editor. I am grateful for the patient and intelligent work he did on behalf of *Lightning at Dinner*.

For JoAnn Verburg

Contents

I

You Are Human

But why not be this lake instead,
icy blue, and the little white curls
of waves, its absolute refusal
to be human? Why not be a thing?

Why not be a place
you'd go to get away
from your mother's frontal lobe eroding
as the faxed medical report has it?

Why not a lovely blue-turning-green
and why not the removal of all feeling?

Maybe she'd rather you be a lake,
a way to lie still in the world,
a melted-down pool of snow,
a place to rest.

You could let yourself wash up on foreign shores.
Or be the surface across which boats might ply their trade,
taking humans from the one shore in sun
to the other side in shade.

You remember humans, don't you?
The ones who row the boat,
who act for all the world
as if they know where they are going?

Brief Lives (I)

An anthology called *Brief Lives*. Not the writings of people who lived briefly, as I had thought. But rather the lives of the famous, written about briefly. It's hard not to admire them. They came, they conquered, they left the scene entirely. Their lives make a sort of graph: perfect.

And the rest of us? Nothing brief about them, these lives of ours: so and so was born. His grandmother befriended him. He hid in lilac bushes. He called Emma Jean Kendell a bad name. He was angry, then afraid. He loved badly, then well, then both at once. His father disappeared in his own time. A cardinal sang. He went to visit his dying mother, letting himself in with his own key. She is taking a shower. He listens to the water running from another room. It has taken them both forever—all their lives—to get to this point. There's no way to be brief, no way to get it over quickly.

Given Your Species

It's something else, the man says, when your daughter at thirteen sits up
    in bed and howls.
Not a nurse comes running: they're used to the sound pain makes inside
    her throat
and not a thing they can give to ease her unless it kills her.

He stands at the head of the bed. She won't have him
hold her hand since the pain only worsens. That's something else, he says,
that's suffering. You can see it one way,

he says, about snow, and call it beautiful, another and call it useful, a
    third way
might be *just stop it,* to beg it to stop falling.

You might, given your species,
want to believe her suffering will end, even now, even while she is alive.
I can't believe it, he says,

how the snow keeps falling: of falling there is more, he says,

then more again. What it is, he says, we are meant to make of such a world,
I don't know, and if I did, I wouldn't say, not even to myself, let alone to
    you
who are my friends, each of you in your own way needing to believe

this is not your life, your daughter, not your species at all.

Release

In prison, I imagined the day of release:
the mountains, the women, dusk
as something you could walk into.
Then it comes at last,
and mainly what you feel is dazed, Mother.
If you're lucky someone embraces you on that day:
is this why you have begun to talk
to your own mother,
dead now twenty years?

In two days, Mother, you'll go away forever
from all you knew was yours.
I'm told it's a good one,
this nursing home. And it's true,
once consigned to hell,
it matters intensely which circle.
They say you'll like the hairdresser
and the physical therapist is so gentle
you'll hardly know you're dying.

On the day of your release,
your prison will lie behind you.
Your own mother will be standing beside your bed then,
stroking your hair, saying over and over,
there now, there now.
At last, it will be true: you are
there now.

Brief Lives (2): Warning

6 A.M., the hour of the serious fishermen
who stand quietly in orange slickers
as they sway slightly in the small boats
far out to sea. Those ancient warnings,
the pelicans, patrol the world closer at hand.
It is the hour when the nurse tries to wake my mother,
then lets her fall back again
into the sea. Some fish are not worth
the keeping. *Asleep again, asleep again,*
her heart rejoices. And the great escape continues,
alone, in darkness, far under the surface.

When I Was a Boy I Was

three gulls before the storm, far out
in the ocean. Their easiness, even though
something difficult is coming.
Surrounded by the vastness
of a life yet to be lived,
I floated in the large wind
of my childhood,
read my books on magic
and threw my ball again and again
into my mother's bed of lilies,
waiting patiently, the good boy I was,
for all that easiness to end.

Pompeii

At the motel, near where the dead
haven't moved in centuries,
there is a pool. A boy carries
a tall lily, as if it is a sacred lamp
the wind could blow out.
His mother sleeps by the pool's edge.
Mama, he calls out,
and louder, *Mama.*
This time she wakes.
The son gives his mother the lily,
then runs away, as if
afraid he will be caught
loving someone that much,
as if the lava is about to flow again
and the only way to stay alive
is to run fast his whole life long,
never stopping, never looking back
at the one face his life has given him
no choice but to love.

Brief Lives (3): Vacation

See how everything is a secret?
his dying mother says to him in the dream.
She had taken the oil, greased her body
and was ready to swim far out,
all the way to the end.
So this is what they mean
by vacation, he thinks to himself,
awake now, looking at the sea.
So this is what they mean:
green, turquoise, silver, the ruin
and rise again of waves,
colors dying inside other colors.

Lighter Now

My mother can name for you
the specific and complicated reasons
cheetahs sleep upstairs.
She can give you a keening
disguised as a polite whisper.
But if it's a little happiness
you want, try someone
a bit farther away
from death. The closer she gets,
the quieter it becomes
inside her head. As if she is listening
to the god over there in the corner,
the one hiding behind the cheetah
who can barely be heard.

I could have gone on loving her
forever, even in her old form,
when everything she said
made a kind of sense, when anger
and bitterness and forgiveness
never got enough
of throwing each other around.
But this is easier yet,
now that she is down to sighs
and those long unpunctuated silences
without beginning or end.

"I see,"
said my mother, without inflection,
after I told her how nice
the nursing home is where soon
she will be continuing,
uninterrupted,

her whispery disappearance
from this earth.

"I am trying to care about
what you are saying,"
she said to me today,
making the effort
to work it out, just exactly
who I am and why
it should matter to her
how much I love being here
in Italy. Cypresses,
I did not bother to say to her,
cypresses appear out of nowhere
just before dawn
to shepherd the night
back down its long aisle,
their needles still wet
with dew, damp and pleasing
to the touch.

What Works for Me

for Mira, age 9

The day's first sparrows work for me,
and bats on summer nights
coming near, then veering away.
And the morning's first suspicious crow—
fearful, greedy—
when it comes slowly cawing down
to its favorite branch.
You point at its glowing eyes
and when it caws three times,
break out laughing.
When the crow flies away,
you look at me astonished,
as if to say, what happens next,
after greed and fear
just give it up and fly away?

Brief Lives (4)

It happens like any other poem,
only snow falls
and at the sight of it,
she smiles.
A woman dying,
yet happy to be alive?
Just try to keep her out of this poem
in which all things
fall together as if one unending
snowstorm. Unending mother:
never be anywhere else
but here.

Someone, Somewhere

loves the world
just as it is.
I fall asleep with that thought.
When I wake up
I feel calm,
as if in my sleep
something had been accomplished
with no effort on my part.

I Don't Think We Need to Know

I don't believe we need to know what below zero feels like.
Or why we die: that, too, I don't think we need to know.
Why life is hard? I think not.

It's hot inside, it's cold out:
that's already a lot to know. That love comes and goes,
that we grow old slowly and then suddenly not.

It helps to know that snow is a god fallen to earth.
Sometimes it helps to let in the world a bit:
some wind, a few flakes, the sound of ice cracking.

Stars, for reasons we'll never know, help show us
who on earth we are and how to bear it here and how
far away we are from knowing why we are small.

Who knows why we love or why we die,
or what exactly wonder is,
demanding that I touch it as if it were the beloved

and I the young bride, believing.

Brief Lives (5): Forgive Him

He simply did not see how the universe opening
inside him was the same as the river inside his mother
unwinding at its own pace, taking her away,
following the only course it knows. He did not see
that even the love he feels for her does not belong to him.
He is of the species that wants to believe in a separate self.
Forgive him this greed, this unending need
to make her life his own.

It Is Not the Fact That I Will Die That I Mind

but that no one will love as I did
the oak tree out my boyhood window,
the mother who set herself
so stubbornly against life,
the sister with her serious frown
and her wish for someone at her side,
the father with his dreamy gaze
and his left hand idly buried
in the fur of his dog.
And the dog herself,
that mournful look and huge appetite,
her need for absolute stillness
in the presence of a bird.
I know how each of them looks
when asleep. And I know how it feels
to fall asleep among them.
No one knows that but me,
no one knows how to love the way I do.

Lightning at Dinner

Basta! shouts the waiter,
then laughs each time the sky
is rent, delighted.
"Such a long journey,"
my failing mother said,
her voice calm and steady,
crossing seven time zones.

Light gone,
you and I sit in the dark. Our hands
touch, finally, hours
after our argument.
This sudden warmth, palm
to palm: as when thunder stops,
the suddenness of all that silence.
Or the aftershock—deafening—
when an only son
is given to understand
his mother's business with him
is completely done.

2

Blood Harmony

I

If there is a god, then the god is not speaking,
only breathing in and out
through the mouth of my mother.
Her repeated rasps
and that small tuneless humming
are all this god has left of her
with which to work,
these and the thick gravel
of her cough, the sound of a gate
being forced:
won't quite close, won't quite open.

I sit in front of what the inevitable will do
to any one of us, how it takes us away
breath by breath.
Listen,
you, God, or whatever
you call yourself now
inside her, pulling her breath in and out:
she was once my mother.

The shy nurse knocks, comes in,
"Is there anything I can get you?"
I say, "No," and she, too, shakes her head,
of course there is nothing to get you.
She closes the door behind her
as she leaves us to our work.
It is not beautiful, this dying,
but it is what this god has for a tool.
And the moon sets
on the last night

God will ever use her
as a way to breathe.

   :::

Mother, I address you now as a victor
speaks to the defeated:
there is a boat hidden down in the harbor.
It has no oars, no motor,
no need of a captain.
It is time now to escape the burning city,
torched beyond recognition.
Let the tide carry you out to sea.
Don't try anything as hopeless
as being. I tell you this as the one
who has spent his life
trying to force happiness on you.
No one will come to your rescue.
Only sky and water now.
Only horizon.

   :::

Outside your window, the lake and the setting moon,
trapped inside the smoke pluming up from the factory,
turning it as gray as your own sinking face,
this day that will take you with it
as it leaves.

   2

Afterwards,
they covered with a simple sheet
the face that had once been
yours and now seemed empty

of the god no longer inside it,
no one ordering you
to continue the cruel, miraculous work
of being.

Almost immediately we left that place
where for two years you had been turned,
one side to the other each day
like an animal roasting, slowly being prepared.

Meanwhile, your grimace still in place,
you lay alone under fluorescent lights
in a room no one ever visits alive
unless they are paid to do so.
Sometime during that long night,
maybe while we ate, maybe later,
while we were washing dishes,
a stranger took away your sheet
to be washed, ironed, and folded.
Then quickly, without ceremony,
you were given to the flames.

3

There is no turning back,
no way to flee to another country.
Gray is the new National Anthem:
what matters now is not what you say,
but to whom you pledge allegiance.
What matters is: do you see her sycamore?
Her cardinals? The moon she swore surprised her
each time?

4

At twelve, I decided I should become a saint.
And now, surely the time has come
to put on brown robes, the rough sandals
only those holier than us
strap to their feet.
Time to look out from the sad, crazed eyes
of grief's holy confusion
onto the cut glass of February sunlight.
And time at long last for the unfamiliar, intriguing scent of self-forgetfulness,
the scent of the earth as it is.

Time to pray to the world as a saint might pray:
once you were my mother, once I was yours.

   :::

The world is beautiful, yet fails its beauty.
What choice, but to love the failings themselves
as she loved the clouds out her hospital window,
mistaking them for birds,
never quite able to remember
their names.
I could hear her tuneless humming
as if, blood harmony, it were also being hummed
inside me, and I saw what my mother saw,
those rain-filled shapes she mistook
for robins, seagulls, sparrows.
Not a god myself,
still I see how it works in heaven:
Birds, she said.

3

Learning a New Language

(Colorado Springs, Colorado)

Last night you sat on the couch
conjugating verbs. I was at the window,
one eye on the dark and untranslatable
stone of the mountain. But the other eye
watched you as you chanted Italian.
I too am learning a verb: to love—
past, present, imperfect, future.
But I keep forgetting how hard it is
to speak a language so foreign
to my tongue. Later,
in bed, you are still reading
from the book of answers.
I fall asleep with the light on,
my back fitting easily into the small cave
of your warmth. I dream you learned
the imperfect, then whispered it
in my ear. The next morning
I wake up first and sit
before the same window.
The world's imperfect beauty
sings its song into my ear.
Out of the darkness,
the mountain rises into light,
untranslatable joy,
happiness in the present tense.

The spread quilt of a humid summer in Umbria.

If there is life after death, it is this.

And she is naked on the bed behind me.

The swallows dipping, then rising again,
refusing to let the sun set all by itself.

Even the whine and rasp of motorcycles.

Even this strange tiredness.

Don't you know where you are?

The pasta is boiling in paradise.

The one dirt road
leads everywhere I need to go.

A naked woman gets up off the bed
and asks, "When do you want to eat dinner?"

The only answer to every question in paradise is

now.

The Chapel Where Giotto Made His Heaven and Hell

(Padua)

A man in heaven walks his dog in a field of daisies,
petals white as fresh linen wrapped around a corpse.
A bearded man in hell never sleeps, exquisitely awake as he is
to the burden he carries, a brown lumpy bundle
strapped to his bent back: heaven and hell
separated by only a few inches.

Late at night, as I get into bed,
the woman already waiting there wonders
which of these two worlds I am in
when I pull back the sheet:
the one with his burden intact, strapped on tight,
or the one just come from the daisy fields,
white linen shroud fresh in mind,
unfinished work still ahead.

It Is the Hour

A small park in Ravenna, a pocket of shade darkening
behind the statue of the general. It is the hour
of tuneless whistling, of serious naps,
of frowning men sitting under pine trees
with thick books, of the girl in her wheelchair,
moaning. It is the hour when you remember the greed
behind your impatience, and the pain it caused,
the hour of remorse, of marigolds
shining their deep yellows and oranges.

Red Poppy, Almost Dark under an Olive Tree

It's only beauty
and of a kind too obvious even to name.
And yet, when you touch me in that way you have,
absentmindedly driving me crazy,
only the red poppy under the olive tree will do,
only stars given chase by sunrise.

Pointless

I don't think swallows were meant to become
emblems of the beloved, absolute capitals
in the alphabet of happiness.

And yet, with swallows
there is no arguing
when it is 3 P.M. by cathedral bells,

though nothing will come
of this happiness,

pointless as the soft ears
of the rabbit carried carefully in its cage
by the woman in dirty blue jeans,

lips downturned, sorrowful and erotic,
as she slept next to her beloved rabbit

on the slow train from Rome to Spoleto, the train
that leaves in the heat of noon, the one no one ever takes.
But we did, you and I, plus two labial rabbit ears

and the anointed lips of a sleeping beauty I will say
is part of my life. Now is not the time to unpack; no, now is the time to love,

as the bells go drifting down,
all the way down to 4 P.M. and counting, they cannot
help themselves.

Teaching the Dog Not to Nip

Do you think it's easy,
not biting
the one you love?
Try loving someone so much
your mouth is only at home
in the place where your teeth
meet the flesh
of your beloved. Try
not tasting the flesh,
not taking in your mouth
the beloved, not
going all the way.

Does He Dare

to use the word *swallows,*
ever again, in a poem?
How they rise and fall, rise once more?
Dare he do it, say swallows and mean
motion changes nothing?
But are they not the very thing,
writing their lives across an empty sky?

What to Write When a Landscape Is Too Beautiful

You do not need to say red poppies,
or even, silver light after rain.
God forgive me all pettiness:
olive trees, olive trees, olive trees.

4

At Night We Read Aloud The Aeneid

But slowly. At this rate,
Rome may never get built.
Each night, the boat of our voices
carries us toward our dreams
on the dissolving tide of a world
both strange and bloody. A world
in which love does not matter,
though our love makes of it
a place we can bear to live.

On the Train to Venice

The first and least important mistake
was to take the train on Sunday, September 1st,
the last day of vacation for millions of Italians.
Though the train was packed,
we had thought to bring sandwiches.
We ate while everyone around us—sitting, standing,
filling every possible inch of floor space—
went profoundly silent and watched
as if we were demonstrating a new technique
for brain surgery, one never tried before,
gone horribly wrong.

Not long after we finished, out of nowhere
came sandwiches, water, and fruit,
every last bit of it offered all around,
especially to those who had brought
nothing with them. Such kindness
and pleasure, such gratitude, except
on the part of the two Americans
who had eaten their fill alone,
in silence, as if the world was empty
of everything but themselves.

Against Empire

Small olives taste best.
Small stars shine farthest.
Small birds call
most sweetly. Small lives,
we are small, small lives.

Soon

It's really over now, summer, I feel
the next thing in the heaviness
of the grapes as they stagger downwards
toward the ripeness
they were born for.
Someone with more power than us
can't take his mind off war.
He wants us to believe power is knowledge.
No one ever told him the truth,
how bewildered he looks, how sad,
and how desperately he seems to long
for danger. Meanwhile, light surrenders
by 6:30 P.M. and rusty barbed-wire fences reappear
where once summer grass covered them
as an ocean covers a treasure sunk long ago.

Not an ounce left of that summer heat that wants of us
only the pleasure of our shirtless company,
no more red poppies like little fragile gods
that have dedicated themselves to ditches
and other lost places where gods
so rarely appear. Yes, the gods have shriveled up
and though the man who sells ice cream in the mercato
still stands behind his chocolate, his lime,
his luscious vanilla and hopes for the best,
in his heart he knows.

Soon the man with the power will point his finger
and husbands will be ordered to put on their uniforms.
Soon, tears and ash, bent heads, fields with the look
of raw wounds, raw wounds with the look
of abandoned fields.

It is the season when olive trees bend heavily
in the cold wind, scraping the ground
as if inviting earth to touch them.
Is it too late for that now? Too late
for one living creature
to touch another? The grandmother
holding the baby by the fountain has no choice
but to remember how happy
it is possible to be. The street cleaner
has the thoughtful brooding look
of a philosopher whose work has been unjustly ignored
for years. He drags his broom behind him
past the drugstore, past the newspaper stand,
past the shadowy boxes loaded down
with oranges from Morocco, cherries from Bari,
walks slowly back and forth across the square
refusing to clean what will only get dirty again.

9/9/02

What It's Like Here

It was nothing unusual. Just a woman, bare-knuckled
on a cold day, pushing an empty grocery cart up University toward hell.
You see it all the time on this planet of theirs.
I had been to what they call a movie. And I was what they call
happy. As you know, fate has given me a wife, beloved to me.
Yes, beloved is a thing they understand. Right now she is playing *come*
with the dog while I write this report. Sometimes she says to me,
"You are really from another planet!" I just hold my tongue.

There is hell around every corner here. There are people who are paid well
to ruin the lives of others. There are people strapped down
to chairs, then a button is pushed. Smoke rises sometimes
off their bodies before they die. I do not tell you this
to shock you, but because you need to know there are planets
where such things happen. Even so, there is happiness
of a kind you would recognize. Right now there is snow,
a thing that divides itself up into many pieces,
then falls from the sky until all ugliness is covered.
"Beautiful day, isn't it," people say and it's not a question.

My question is, "Where do I go from here? What do you want of me?
Why was I born on this planet?" You'll want to know, did I stop
and help the lady. I did not. And you'll want to know
what does "beloved" mean, if not that. I don't know. I only breathe
one breath at a time. Not like you who breathe so many lives
at once. We drove home, my beloved and I. The movie?
It was called *Men of Honor,* a kind of dream
of how things should be. We didn't like it.
Nothing about it rang true. But we held hands anyway,
then went out into the bare-knuckled cold, described above.

Christ Resurrected

The miracle is not that he came back,
but that he was willing
to leave behind such stillness,
and so recently achieved.

Self-Portrait Doing T'ai Chi in Chinatown, 7 A.M.

                              Slowly
I turn my hips, as if
sex is my true country
and the poise of it
spreads evenly everywhere
blood flows.
                              Everything
must be done just so,
as in a dream when one ascends,
                              then flies,
leaving it all behind.
And the Lower East Side
reveals itself, from above, as a river
of lives unwinding toward the sea
into which, one day,
all of us will have slipped
                              quite easily.

                    There is a statue
they call Liberty. Countrymen,
it is a beautiful idea,
a woman rising from the water
bearing light.

                    Such thoughts
I think inside the slow hula
my body makes
                         of its need

to be silent,

                      to move

with such fluid precision,

                      to know

what it means to be of this world,

                      while flying

ever so slowly towards the next.

It

We are not it, but it requires us.
It does not accept this century or the last. It hasn't the taste
for starvation or gas. It is not a rooster,
but it loves the way the rooster needs everyone to know:
this day is made for roosters: do not lose all hope.

Last Night at Dinner

Someone is back with us,
someone who almost died.
I'm the bald one. I smile
and pass him the noodles. Can anyone
ever see all the way inside us?
Someone sits at eye level
across the table from me.
Our fathers died,
each in their own time.

An orange light hovers
over the clouded city,
though it's dark
and has been for hours.
As if somewhere a fire rages
out of control,
and we are its kindling.

The fish we eat is firm
and sweet. The son
of my friend charges a quarter
for his father to enter his room:
a bargain!
There is a secret life inside us
that knows the cost,
that is willing to pay the price.

When the Dog Is Sick

She eats white rice,
white rice only.
Little Buddha with your curved smile
of a tail, tell me
what life is like
for those who love
without condition or restraint.

Get Used to It, Being

The day after the Day of the Dead
where do you put the bones
you don't need, the paint, the wig, the circles
in black around the eyes, the dead-white flesh?

I don't mind the dead,
when they are not yet fully grown,

knocking politely at the door. They want
a little sweetness, arriving costumed
in the skirt of not-being, wearing the smeared cape
that drapes what is and reveals what is not.

Trick or treat! Give or be soaped!
In greed and fear, in death's near light,
in need: get used to it, being.

The dead stand at the door and hold out their bowls,
little monks begging for more life;
and this one night we do not turn away
from how the dead need us to come to the door

and smile. We say, good costume, we say,
what can we give you from our still warm hands?

5

It Is Hard Not to Love the World

but possible. When I am like this,
even the swallows are not God.
Even the yellow school bus.
Even the children inside,
wanting out, are not God.

Happiness

Uncle Vanya was sad last night, so bitter, bewildered and trapped, just like every other time I've seen him. "In two hundred years," he said, "perhaps they will have discovered how to be happy." Well, it didn't take that long. We know now that happiness is sitting in darkened theaters and watching failed worlds beautifully acted: the love affairs that turn ridiculous and the drunken impoverished dreams, the wistful hopes, and the fleeting moments of grace.

What happiness to go back again to the staged rainy night, the lightning, the sound of the revolver. Back to the dark and passionate purposes of love, the birch forest, the relief of experiencing a dreariness suffered through by someone else, then left when we walk out, after the play is finished, into the cold fall air. What happiness to know that all our mistakes have been made before, have been made over and over on one stage or another for at least one hundred twenty-five years. And then, too, the small moments of tenderness: whether acknowledged or not on stage, we in the audience saw them. Those dear familiar bald heads of the men, the hair turning white on the women. And the same pointless jokes, and the hearts, the same broken hearts. All that love and all that loneliness. Let the thunder begin, let the curtain rise.

Giotto's Resurrection *in San Croce*

(Florence)

When what stands guard falls asleep,
only then can the new arise.
How beautiful the soldier in green as he sleeps,
arms thrown back, warding off light.
You recognize that posture from your own naps,
the body's giving in to your need to leave this world.

A beautiful woman beats on her drum
when you nap today
just for you.
How serious she is, how perfectly
her red sandals match the red of her drum.
The heartbeat she makes is as regular and comforting
as music. When you wake
you're no god brought back to life,
but a man whose own life is resurrected
one drum beat at a time.

Crickets Well Begun

Here come those swallows yet again,
50s jazz from the terrace up above,
curl of cigarette smoke a table away
where the young man with the earring
holds forth to the young man with the earring,
crickets well begun, figs
at lunch, the boredom
now that there is nothing
not to love, quiet darkness coming,
Remembrance of Things Past
waiting on the cardboard box,
the mountains holding their blues
against the sky, the years going faster now,
and now tiredness like the hand of a lost brother,
heavy on my shoulder, so sure of its rights,
he's long overdue, the absent one, now come home at last.

Late / Later / Latest

If I stood like this each evening near nightfall,
stood silent in June next to this olive tree,
if I could breathe in time to its breathing,
to the in of fading light, the out of oncoming darkness,
what fear could death then hold for me?

Strange World

In the life before this one,
these evergreens
draped
with a thickly needled hush,
these bearers of fragrant shadows
smelling faintly of another world
as babies do after their bath—
in the life before this one,
these trees were hermits
who prayed steadily
through the long nights of self-hatred
and the even longer days
filled with wearisome unending fear.

Because of their stubborn devotion
to the invisible god
in which they believed
despite all lack of evidence,
they were allowed to come back
rooted in the deep earth of humility,
this time unafraid of the darkness
or the light.

Now they no longer need
to pray with words:
their whole bodies rise up
in thick-barked praise,
in needles shaking with delight,
even as they sink down
into secret black rivers
of roots
which circle the earth
in a slow measured flowing

unbothered
by the great triumphs
that occur on earth,
or the even greater failures.

We are not such marvelous hermits
and never will be.
These trees are from god.
And if it turns out there is no god,
still they have found a way
to come from him.
Strange and pitiable world—
it is still possible
for us to walk by an evergreen
and not bow our heads in prayer
as we would bow our heads
before any god
suddenly put in our path,
any god
singing of heaven and earth,
of darkness and light,
of the world to come
and the world that has always been.

At Least

Since it seems the consensus that one day I must die,
seems all my friends, too, will go,
at least let there be thunder on that day.
And the steady comfort of a summer rain.
Since sound, they say, is the last thing to fail.

Let it be so. But if it cannot be,
if the season is bare of leaves, the death painful
and greed for the world still fiercely with us,
then let someone else be allowed our place on the white couch,
rain falling, the final sounds of a life listened to
and, without fear, let go of, listened to and let go of.

On That Day

Perhaps on the day time leaves me behind
like an earring
slipped behind a couch,
perhaps on that day: calm and humility.
But probably not. Probably, mostly fear.
Probably a long summer dusk,
swallows followed by bats.
If I'm lucky, an extra quilt
to throw over me at the last moment
because the nights are chilly here
and it is good to sleep the night through without waking.

Seven Invisible Strings

1

I remember my mother toward the end,

    folding the tablecloth after dinner
        so carefully,
    as if it were the flag
        of a country that no longer existed,
    but once had ruled the world.

2

Almost 8 A.M., curtain drawn shut, lying in bed, naked:

      it's not the same as sex,
    but close
        as a door slams,
    a shoe crunches on gravel,
        walking away.
    Then the long afterwards of lying still—
        happy, lonely,
    who can say which—
        the world
    just as it is, and the lover, too,
        just so.

3

This spring night,

     everyone at the party
younger than me
     except for one man.
We give each other the secret password.

4

On this cloudy May day,

     I keep thinking
maybe June is what I need
     to make me happy.

5

Tears? Of course, but also the marsh grass

     near the Mississippi:
your whispers and mine,
     and the dog's long contented sighs.

6

Helicopter flies overhead

 reminding me of that old war
  where one friend lost his life,
 one his mind,
  and one came back happy
 to be missing only an unnecessary finger.

7

Almost sixty:

 from now on
  even begonias are amazing.

What Do I Look Like?

Clusters of dandelion seeds,

spent and beautiful,
casting themselves without worry or fear
into the very current of air that carries them away from themselves.

I have taken a shape
that loses itself in the wind, a common weed, without parent or child.
Everywhere I land, I feather again,
again begin without regard to beauty.

What do I look like?

This lilac-scented, windblown, gauzy, cardinal-throated spring.
No one need bother tell me ever again
what's up ahead.

As the purple lilacs feel, swollen and full, asway on their bent stems,
so I feel when someone picks me in huge handfuls,
puts me in water and keeps me for as long as I last.

JIM MOORE is the author of five previous collections of poetry, including *The Freedom of History* and *The Long Experience of Love*. His poems have appeared in *American Poetry Review*, the *Nation*, the *New Yorker*, the *Paris Review*, the *Threepenny Review*, the *Pushcart Prize Anthology*, and in many other magazines and anthologies. Moore has received numerous awards and fellowships from the Bush Foundation, The Loft, the McKnight Foundation, and the Minnesota State Arts Board. He teaches at Hamline University in Saint Paul, Minnesota, and at The Colorado College in Colorado Springs, as well as online through the University of Minnesota Split Rock Arts Program. He is married to the photographer JoAnn Verburg. They live in Saint Paul, Minnesota and Spoleto, Italy.

The text of *Lightning at Dinner* has been set in Clifford, a typeface designed by Akira Kobayashi. Book design by Wendy Holdman. Composition by Stanton Publication Services, Inc. Manufactured by Bang Printing on acid-free paper.